paper punch art

Create more than 200 easy designs with the punches and paper shapes inside!

by Laura Torres

★ American Girl™

Published by Pleasant Company Publications
Copyright © 2001 by American Girl, LLC

Questions or comments? Call 1-800-845-0005, visit our Web site at **americangirl.com**,
or write to Customer Service, American Girl, 8400 Fairway Place, Middleton, WI 53562-0497.

Printed in China. Punches made in China.

06 07 08 09 10 LEO 10 9 8 7 6 5 4 3 2 1

Editorial Development: Trula Magruder, Michelle Watkins
Design: Mengwan Lin
Production: Kendra Pulvermacher, Janette Sowinski
Photography: James Young
Styling: Jessica Hastreiter, Mengwan Lin, Sarajane Lien, Trula Magruder, Jinger Peissig,
Kendra Pulvermacher, Laura Torres

Grab the glue, pull out the punch packets, and pick out a design. That's all you need to do to start making **paper punch** art.

Inside, you'll learn how to create pets, places, people, and more. You'll also **find projects** to give as presents or to display in your room.

Most of the art is **so simple,** you won't need directions. Just look closely at the punched shape, and you'll see how to **do it yourself.**

Happy punching!

letter to you

getting started

you will need

All the designs in this book were made using just the punched shapes in your kit. The other supplies you will need are paper, a small pair of scissors, toothpicks, wax paper, aluminum foil, and glue. Sometimes you'll need a regular paper punch to cut tiny circles out of other punched shapes.

Your kit includes a heart and a star punch. You'll need these to create a couple of the bookmark crafts shown inside. If you run out of the circle or swirl shapes, look for these punches at craft or scrapbook stores—or get creative and try the punches you have at home!

make it stick!

Punched shapes don't need a lot of glue to stay in place. Squeeze a small amount of white glue onto a piece of paper. Dip a toothpick in the glue, and spread a thin layer of it on the back of the punched shape. You can use your sticky toothpick to pick up and place your punched shapes.

Glue

know your punches

If your new punches are stiff, break them in by punching through a few layers of wax paper a couple of times. Do this occasionally to keep punches working smoothly. If a punch dulls after frequent use, punch through aluminum foil to sharpen it. Store punches in a cool, dry place.

sneaky shapes

With a few snips of the scissors, you can turn punched shapes into other shapes.

Cut a heart in half to make teardrops. Use teardrops for flower petals or insect wings.

The points on a star make small triangles—good for noses, bird feet, and beaks.

Cut circles in half for leaves, boats, and turtle shells.

Cut and flip-flop a swirl to make long, wavy lines for sun rays, vines, and more!

sky's the limit!

Overlap circles as you glue them down in an arc.

Cut out a body with scissors. Cut hearts in half for wings.

Tail feathers are pieces of swirl. Wings are heart halves. Snip a triangle out of a circle to make a beak.

Find a ● for the head and a ● for the body. Use a ♥ for the tail and a ♥ cut in half for the wings. Cut tips from a ☆ for the beak and feet.

Find ◎◎. Use a ◎ for the center of the sun. Cut the other ◎ into pieces for the rays.

Cut 1 point off a ★. Clip the rest of the ★ in half for wings. Cut a strip of paper for the body. Draw antennae with a marker.

be mine

Find some hearts in 2 colors.
Cut them in half. Switch halves.

Happy
♥ Valentine's ♥
Day!♥

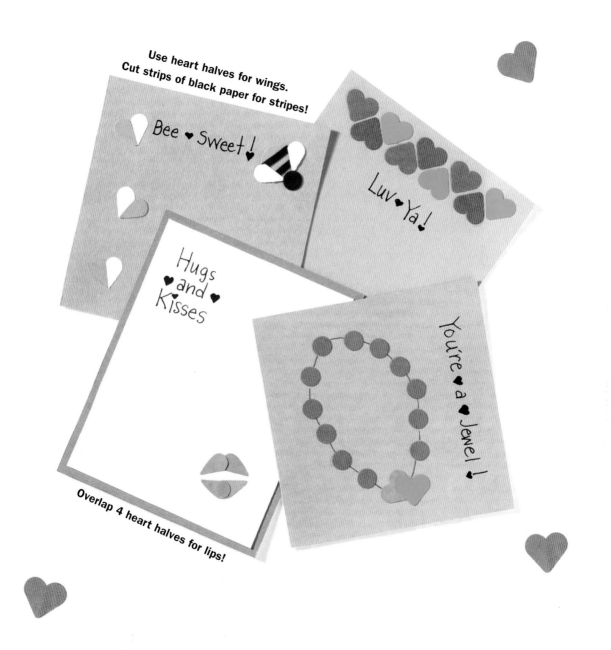

Use heart halves for wings.
Cut strips of black paper for stripes!

Bee ♥ Sweet! ♥

Luv ♥ Ya! ♥

Hugs
♥ and ♥
Kisses

You're ♥ a ♥ Jewel! ♥

Overlap 4 heart halves for lips!

field of flowers

lacy rose

Find ⵌⵌⵌⵌⵌ. Glue the outer end of 1 swirl to the inside end of another. Repeat until all swirls are connected into a flower. Add a ● to the center. For the stem, connect the outer ends of ⵌⵌ.

fancy phlox

Glue the points of ♥♥♥♥♥ around a ○. Glue a ○ onto each ♥, as shown. Center 2 overlapping ★★. Finish with a ●.

pretty pansies

For each flower, glue ♥♥♥ so that the points touch. Add overlapping ●●● on top, then a ● center. Use a ⵌ for each stem.

petite poppies

For each flower, use scissors to fringe ●. Add a ● to the center. Cut a strip of paper for a stem, and add half a ◑ for a leaf.

in the garden

Use hearts and circles for wings.

Use half-circles or heart halves for bee wings.

a closer look

Start with a ● body. Cut a tiny white square for the tooth. Glue it onto an upside-down ♥ to make the head. Use a ★ point for a nose, ♥♥ for legs, and ♥♥ halves for paws and ears.

Cut a ♥ in half. Use the rounded top of one half for the head and the point of the other half for the tail. A @ over a ● makes a shell.

Glue a ● to a ● for the head and body. Add a ◐ cut in half. Glue ●● on top.

card for mom

To make this Mother's Day card or a card for any other occasion, you'll need a regular paper punch. For each flower, find ●●●●●. Nip a piece from each ● with the regular punch. Overlap the ●s as you glue them down. Add a ★ on top. Cut a paper stem, and then cut a ♥ in half for leaves.

birthday card

To make this card, start with the cake. Use scissors to cut 2 rectangles, one smaller than the other. Glue them onto a card, as shown. Find lots of ♥s and glue them upside-down for icing. Add candles, balloons, and confetti.

candles

For each candle, cut a ♥ in half. Flip the halves so that they fit together to form the candle. Use a ♥ half for a flame.

balloons

For each balloon, use a ●. Cut off a ★ point, then glue the top of the point under the ●. Use a marker to draw a string.

a closer look

Glue down a ⬤ for a body and a ⬤ for a head. Cut a ★ point for a tail. Cut a ♥ in half for ears. Use a ⚪ for a spot, a ⬤ for a muzzle, and ⬤⬤ for legs. Draw eyes and a nose with a marker.

Glue overlapping ⚪⚪ for a body and head. Add ⚪⚪⚪⚪ for paws. The ears are ★ points, the nose is a point cut off a ♥, and the tail is a piece of a ⚬.

Cut a ⚬ in sections. Flip-flop pieces to make a wavy hose. Add a paper rectangle for a nozzle.

For hair, glue small whole and half-circles to a large circle head. For the shirt, start with a whole star and add star sections. To make a leg, cut the edges off a heart and glue the edges together. Repeat for the other leg.

Cut a large paper trunk with scissors. For the tire swing, use a large circle, then place a smaller circle within it.

furry friends

Spot

everlasting eggs

Paint wooden eggs in various colors with acrylic paint. Make your punch art first, then use a strong craft glue to stick the art in one piece onto the egg. Display the eggs at Easter, in spring, or at any time of year!

hopping bunny

Overlap ◯◯ for the body and head. Cut ♡♡♡ in half, using 2 halves for ears and 3 for legs. Use ◯◯◯ for cheeks and a tail. Snip the bottom of a ♥ for a nose.

dinky duck

Trim a ⬤, then glue the larger piece down. Add a ● for the head. Use half of a ● for feet and half of a ♥ for a wing. Cut off a ★ point for a beak.

sweet sheep

Glue down lots of overlapping ◯s for a body, a ● for a head, ●● for feet, and a ♥ cut in half for ears.

a picnic

tasty tacos

Find a ● shell and fold it in half. Inside, glue a ● for meat, ★ pieces for lettuce, and a half ◖ for tomato. Glue the taco in place.

burger and fries

For a hamburger, glue down a ●, then add ★ lettuce, ● tomato, and a ● burger. Top with another ●. For fries, lay ◯◯ on top of each other. With scissors, cut off the sides of both circles and the top of the front circle only. Cut a ● into strips. Glue the fries inside the package.

fancy fruit

For a lime (or lemon) slice, stack  so that thin layers of white and dark green (or yellow) show on one edge. Cut in half. For a strawberry, place ⭐ points on a ♥. For an apple, cut a 🌑 and a 🌕 in half and layer them. Use a regular punch to make a bite. Add fruit seeds with a marker.

sweet snacks

For chocolate-chip cookies, punch the edge off a ⚫ with a regular punch. Add marker chips! For sandwich cookies, layer ●○●. For a sundae, punch ●○○ ice cream. Hand-cut a cherry. Cut a 🌑 in half for the dish and turn the bottom of a 💛 upside-down for the base.

a small sip

Trim 2 sides off a 🌑 to make a glass. For milk, cut another 🌑 a little smaller than the glass. Use a regular punch to curve in the top. Cut a straw with scissors.

pond life

Make wings with fancy paper.

Turtle heads and tails are heart halves.

Use large and small half-circles to make lily pads.

Use hearts for knobby legs and layered small circles for buggy eyes.

Stars make perfect frog feet.

Use swirl pieces and
layered hearts for graceful swans.

frame it!

Decorate photo frames or colorful pre-cut mats with paper punch art. Try this mistake-proof method: first create flowers, insects, and patterns. Then lay out your design before gluing the art to the frame or mat.

patterns

To make the back frame, use ⬤s and ⬤s in many different colors. Glue a ⬤ to each ⬤, mixing the colors, then glue them all together into a large circle. Place 1 circle in each corner of the frame. Accent with ⬤s.

springtime

Make 3 daisies, and glue them in a row across the front of a paper frame. To make a flying insect, cut a body from paper. For wings, cut a ◖ in half, or cut ❤ ❤ in half. Use ☺☺ for swirling wind!

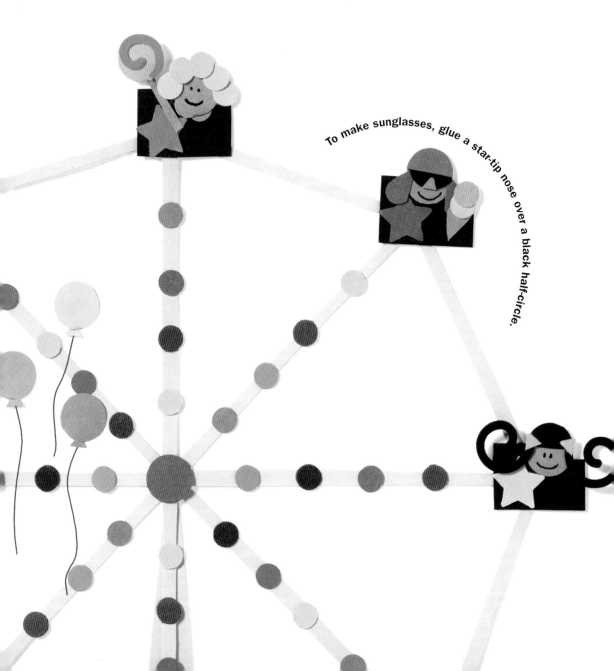

To make sunglasses, glue a star-tip nose over a black half-circle.

Make bears from large and small circles.

For a hat, cut a ◖ in half, then punch off the top with a regular punch. Cut a small strip for a hatband. Glue ♥ halves point-to-point for a brim.

For cars, glue a ◯ cut in half for the hood and trunk. Use half a ◯ for the cab. A window is half of a ◯.

Use heart halves to make this girl's arms and legs. Overlap 2 hearts for a skirt.

scrapbook

Friends

Jenna, Chelsea & Kaylie:
Three amigos at the
annual school picnic!

Here we are
close to nature!

SUMMER

Lizzie and Ashley were a big splash at camp!

Cut an arc around 2 points of a star to make a body. A swirl with a small circle makes a bushy tail. Ears are star points.

CAMP

Cut a heart in half for ears. Overlap small circles for feathers, then add the bottom of a heart behind the eyes. Half a heart makes a beak.

Sneaking in a late-night snack!

ocean view

Use a star with 2 points cut off for a tail.
Create fish lips with half a circle.

To make crab claws, use swirls and small circles.

To make a sail, cut the top off a heart.

Make these 8 legs with pieces of swirl.

Layer small circles for the mermaid's body and scales.
Use heart halves for fins and pieces of swirl for arms.

the mighty jungle

Elephant legs are star points. The tail and trunk are pieces of swirl.

For the panda's face, find a large white circle. Add 4 small black circles for eyes and ears. Punch the edge off a large white circle for a lemon-shaped muzzle. The nose is a star point.

Monkey legs are heart halves. Arms are pieces of swirl.

This star-faced fox has legs made from a small circle and hearts cut in half.

Punch the edges off large circles to make bananas.

Fringe a green paper strip, then glue it to an orange rectangle. Add flowers made from stars and circles.

Cut out purple triangles, and punch a heart from the tip of each one. Glue triangles on top of an orange rectangle, as shown. Add heart halves to make butterfly wings and bodies.

bookmarks

Cut 2 different-colored rectangles the same size. Punch stars from one, then glue the rectangles together. Add sweet words for charm.

When you wish upon a star, your dreams come true ☆ When you wish upon a star, your dreams

Let heart-winged butterflies and flowers shaped from overlapping circles drift over a purple field.

fall fun

Clip stars in half for bat wings. Make a heart body and a small circle head. Add star points for ears.

To make each pumpkin, glue 2 large half-circles behind another large circle. Use swirls for a leafy vine.

For trick-or-treater's shirt, cut the sides off a large circle and use heart halves for sleeves

For black widow's legs, use swirl pieces.

Come have
some
Wicked
fun!

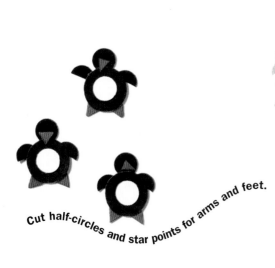

Glue down a heart, then overlap large circles. Add an upside-down heart. Half-circles make tusks, and heart halves make flippers.

Cut half-circles and star points for arms and feet.

Heart halves and half-circles make legs and feet. Cut a piece of a star for a head.

To make a head, glue small circles around a large circle. For a body, cut the sides off a large circle. Arms and legs are half-circles and heart halves.

To: Dad
From: Anna

From: Anna
To: Mom

To: Kaylee
From: Anna

To: Josh
From: Anna

gift tags

To:
Jessie
From:
Anna

To: Aunt Sue From: Anna

To: Grandma
From:
Anna

Cut the edge off a heart to make a mitten. Add half-circle cuffs.

To: Michelle
From: Anna

lights out

To make an owl's crest, cut off the top of a heart.

Want to wow us with your paper-punch project?

Send it in!

Write to:
Paper Punch Art Editor
American Girl
8400 Fairway Place
Middleton, WI 53562

Sorry! Photos and projects cannot be returned.

**All comments and suggestions received
by American Girl may be used without
compensation or acknowledgment.**

Here are some other American Girl books you might like:

❑ I read it.

❑ I read it.

❑ I read it.

❑ I read it.